CORRIDORS OF POWER

The Enemy Within

CORRIDORS OF POWER

The Enemy Within

William T Lovatt

ATHENA PRESS
LONDON

First Published 2006 by
ATHENA PRESS
Queen's House, 2 Holly Road
Twickenham TW1 4EG
United Kingdom

Printed for Athena Press

Contents

The Beginning…

I WAS BORN in Newcastle-under-Lyme on 17 September 1928, the youngest of four children born to Tom and May Lovatt. I was born into poverty and deprivation, but was fortunate to have loving and caring parents. Having experienced extreme poverty first-hand, I promised myself that when I grew up I would make every effort to eradicate poverty and hardship amongst the working classes.

My father served in the Royal Marines and was also a miner at this point. Later he became an industrial engineer. My mother was a devoted wife and mother. She occupied her time as a busy housewife, raising the family.

I attended Rye Croft School in Newcastle, later moving on to Knutton Secondary Modern, where I remained until I was thirteen years and seven months old.

On leaving school, I took up employment in the local coal mine, but it being hard and dirty work, I soon realised that this was not what I wanted to do.

On leaving the mines, I took up various jobs in the building trade and finally became a lorry driver.

In October 1946 I was called upon to do National Service and served with REM/R/Signals and Panas Special Ops Wireless Operatex, serving in Europe, the Middle East and the Far East throughout the war. I signed on for extra service after peace was declared and was eventually demobbed in July 1954, when I returned to Civvy Street and the building trade.

In 1955 I joined Stoke-on-Trent ambulance service, and eventually retired in 1989. During my time in the ambulance service I became involved with the Union NUPE, becoming

Branch Secretary upon my retirement. My union work brought me into contact with many organisations.

In 1957 I joined the local Labour Party and served as a local councillor for some fifteen years, enabling me to pursue my ambition to improve living standards for the working classes. I very quickly made my mark on local policies, chairing most major committees of the council. My determination and refusal to compromise my ideals made me very few friends and many enemies, but I always stood up for what I believed in…

Medical Records

I WAS AT WORK one day when I was summoned to the telephone by a member of staff, who informed me it was a lady asking especially for me. The caller, who I identified as Miss J H, receptionist at the local Accident and Emergency department, sounded very upset. I decided it would be best if we met to discuss the problem face to face in my capacity as a Union official.

Miss H informed me she had been sacked for allegedly destroying medical records, breach of confidentiality and drug addiction. She was not a member of any trade union, but alleged she had been dismissed unfairly. I agreed to make inquiries and report back.

My first task was to see the hospital secretary, Mr Carter, who was involved with the case. It soon became clear to me that there was something far more serious going on: a witch hunt against a senior consultant. Miss H was being made a scapegoat in order to get back at the consultant. It appeared she had carried out some private work for the consultant in question. However, having interviewed staff who had worked with Miss H, it became clear to me that they had been warned not to say anything or they would lose their jobs.

My next step was to set up an appeal for the reinstatement of Miss H. This was held at local level with a panel of three senior officers of the Local Health Authority. At the beginning of this enquiry there were no fewer then twelve senior officers of the Health Authority involved.

After two days of debating, needless to say, the appeal was lost as the Authority closed ranks to protect itself.

Having explored all avenues locally, I had failed to see the lady reinstated.

I was then approached by Mr Mitting – an orthopaedic surgeon who had discovered that medical records were going missing at around this time. He wanted me to join forces with him, as he was getting nowhere and suspected he was being persecuted by the Local Health Authority as a result of his investigations. This seemed to support Miss H's claims…

My next move was to appeal to the Birmingham Regional Health Authority, chaired by Sir David Perris, against the dismissal of Miss H. Needless to say I lost the appeal again.

As a result of pushing this matter, I was subjected to threats, persecution, intimidation, loss of reputation and at one stage I have reason to believe a contract was taken out on my life as I was getting too close to the truth involving senior officers of the Authority. Mr Mitting, because of his movements and involvement, experienced similar treatment.

However, this only made me more determined to carry on.

Being a local councillor, I enlisted the support of my MP, Mr Stephen Swingher, asking him to raise the matter in the House of Commons. I also appealed to the House of Lords for their intervention.

Finally, the matter was raised on *Prime Minister's Question Time*. Within twenty-four hours, I was summoned to a meeting in Birmingham where I was threatened by the chairman, who told me to drop the matter as I was hunting a lot of good people. I was later informed by the House of Commons that my member would be fully reinstated to her former position, with immediate effect.

However, on returning to work, Miss H found herself placed in a junior position, filing records. I immediately took the matter to the Authority. It took twelve months to put matters right.

During this time, Miss H, Mr Mitting and myself suffered terrible abuse and character assassination.

The whole inquiry took no less then seven years and cost the Authority one million pounds. All the officers involved either resigned or were demoted and moved to other areas.

Having been appointed a magistrate in 1962, I again found myself subjected to abuse and threats during the course of meetings when I refused to compromise my beliefs, though I refused to be intimidated…

Judiciary

BECAUSE OF MY involvement with the medical records saga, I was asked to attend a meeting with the chairman and clerk to the magistrates.

It was alleged that I was having an affair with a married woman, a nurse whom I had known through my trade union activities. I was also accused of forging her name in the local electoral register, by pretending that she was Mrs Lovatt, my spouse. I was still married with two young children at the time. I was given the option to resign or I would face criminal proceedings. I refused to resign and informed the chairman that I would fight the case to clear the lady's name and restore my own unblemished character.

I eventually ended up with the Lord Chancellor's representative, who informed me that, owing to my political and union activities, I had made a lot of enemies and the charges against me were unfounded and nothing more than an attempt at character assassination. I was to resume my full magistrate's duties. This I did until I retired in 1998.

Contract to Kill

ONGOING BATTLES with the Local Health Authority continued to cause me aggravation. Having teamed up with the senior consultant orthopaedic Mr A K Mitting, who had come to me with complaints about medical records at the time of Miss Humphries' dismissal – i.e. that he was unable to operate on his patients due to inadequate annotation – my life was now in danger.

Between us we investigated numerous complaints from patients and staff that medical records were being misplaced and lost. On one occasion I discovered a pile of notes in a disused garage belonging to the Authority some five miles from where they should have been.

Things got worse and I was once

again subject to threats and intimidation. Mr Mitting and I were followed everywhere we went. I later discovered there was a contract out to kill both of us. On one occasion the assassins almost succeeded as I was leaving a public house one evening. I was targeted by two villains and was lucky to escape unhurt.

Ambulance Service

IN THE COURSE of my trade union activities, as secretary for National Union Public Employees I was asked by the chief ambulance officer to attend a meeting at HQ Stafford. Here I was informed that the Authority were considering closing down the Stoke-on-Trent ambulance control centre and moving everything to Stafford.

I informed the CAO I was totally opposed to the proposal and that I would mount a public campaign to overturn this decision. The campaign lasted for twelve years: petitions, meetings with the Local Authority; peaceful demonstrations; radio and TV coverage, etc.

During all this time I was subjected to abuse and dismissed three times for neglect of duty and incompetence. I thought this was all very familiar – it was like the medical records debacle all over again.

The final decision was made by the government, and came in 1988. It was decided to close down the Stoke-on-Trent control and move everything to Stafford. I refused to go and opted for redundancy.

Although it took twelve years, I am proud to have been involved in this campaign; I fought and lost, but what an experience it was.

Incidentally, the service has not improved for the people of Stoke-on-Trent, as we were promised.

Local Authority Membership

As I've mentioned, I was elected on the council of Newcastle-under-Lyme in 1972 and retired in 1988.

During my time as councillor I held almost every office there was and I made a lot of enemies.

I was subjected to character assassination by fellow councillors because of my union activities; accusations made against me included the claim that I neglected my children and that I was a womaniser who had had a string of affairs with married women. These were both proved to be false.

At the time I was living in a council house with my family – my wife and two children. My wife was very vulnerable and believed all the slander against me. Our marriage broke up in 1972.

Although we were divorced, I continued to live under the same roof as my former wife as I refused to leave the matrimonial home. The council eventually issued an order to evict me as a bad tenant on the basis of my being a divorcee, thus making me homeless.

Having informed the council that I would appeal against this injustice, it took some twelve months to reverse their decision to evict me. It was resolved that I would remain in the matrimonial home and my wife would be rehoused to a property of her choice. It was also ruled that the council would never again evict a person simply because of divorce proceedings. This policy is now the norm for all Local Authorities, so while I suffered, at least it had a positive effect in the long term.

At the time of this dispute a Mr C Moreton was town clerk for the Authority. He asked me to call on him and I explained the position I found myself in. He apologised on behalf of the council and informed me that the council, through some of its senior members, had embarked on character assassination merely to get me to resign my position.

It appears I had hurt a lot of people and was getting too near the truth about the activities of certain members and so was persecuted mercilessly.

Capital Punishment

IT WAS A COLD and dark night as I was preparing to attend a local council meeting. The main item for discussion was the restoration or otherwise of the death penalty for murder. I was strongly opposed to the death penalty and would speak on the matter to the council. There were a number of members who were determined, come what may, to bring back capital punishment. It was going to be a gritty discussion and a very close vote.

I spoke at great length on the matter and moved for the status quo to remain. The vote finally put, the resolution was lost and my motion was carried.

Meeting concluded, I proceeded to the local pub, whereupon I was accosted by a group of people aided by

none other than the 'bring back hang-
ing' mob, shouting and hurling abuse
at me.

'We'll get you for this!' they shouted
– a threat to destroy my political ca-
reer…

Bribery

I WAS ATTENDING a council meeting one afternoon when the clerk to the town hall informed me there was a gentleman in the main entrance wishing to see me.

The gentleman was a local builder who had submitted a planning application to build seventy-six houses on a plot of land falling under my jurisdiction. I interviewed the gentleman and it transpired that he wished to give me a brand new dwelling, provided the planning application went through: a bribe.

Incidentally, as chairman of the planning permission committee, I had recommended only thirty-four dwellings be built on this particular site, a decision which had been accepted by the council. It was decided that no action would be taken against the builder, but I accompanied the town clerk to give him a severe warning.

Shortly after this incident, my wife, Ruth, was disturbed one evening by someone at the front door of the house. Being on her own, Ruth was reluctant to see who was out there, or what the noise was. It appeared someone had left a parcel on the doorstep containing of a piece of very expensive Royal Doulton pottery.

I returned home late that evening, surprised to see Ruth still waiting up for me as she normally retired to bed early. She wanted an explanation from me as to why someone would leave expensive pottery on her doorstep.

It became clear that a local garage owner, who had applied for a change of use planning application for his car showrooms had left the pottery as a bribe to lure me into granting permission for the change of use.

The unwanted gift was returned to

its owner, who was rebuked by the town clerk. Nothing more was heard of this incident, but some time later I found out that it was a set-up organised by certain council members to implicate me in their shady dealings.

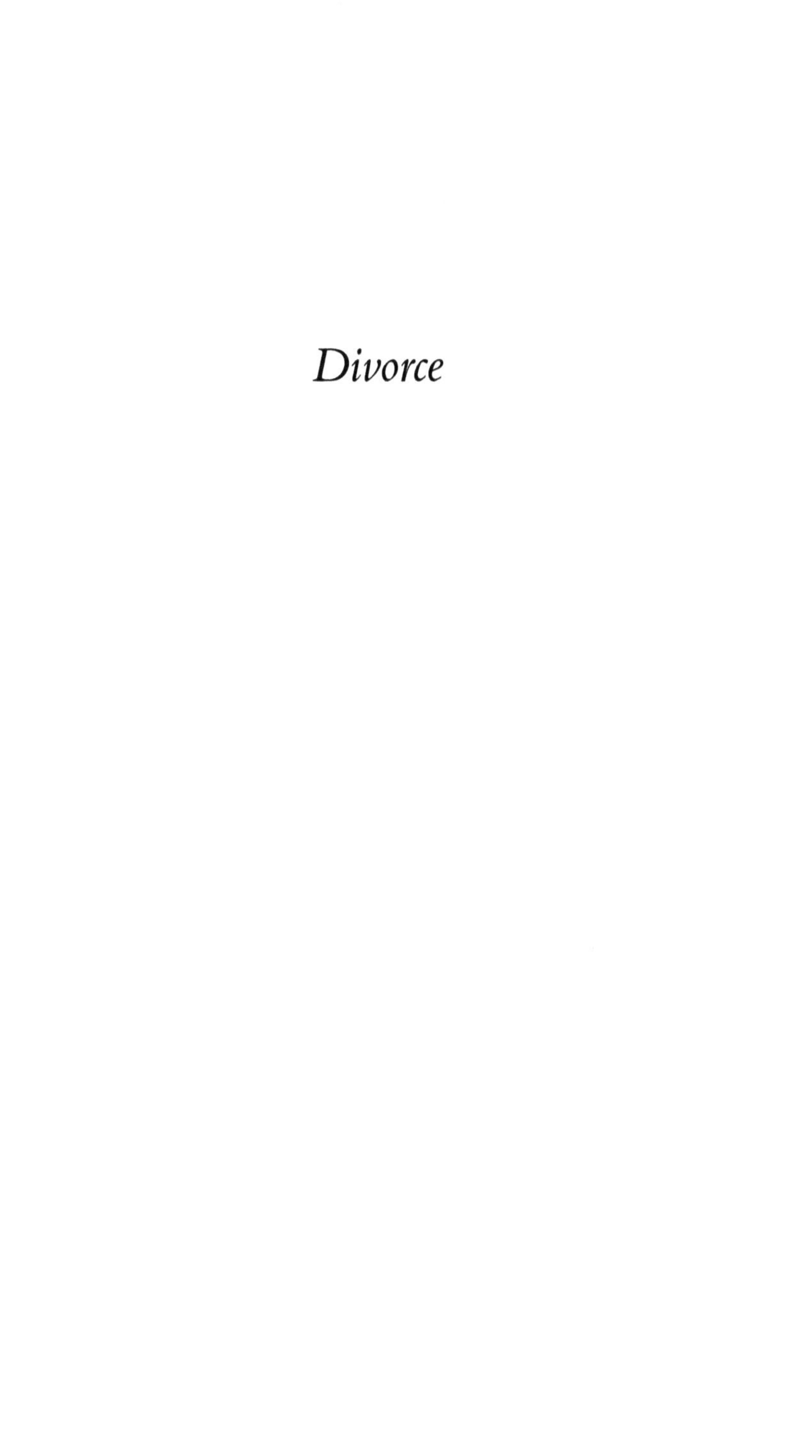

Divorce

ONE AFTERNOON I was relaxing at home when the doorbell rang. Being on my own at the time, I answered the door. I was confronted by a gentleman dressed in a black bowler hat and carrying a briefcase. Having identified me as the person he was seeking, the gentleman produced a document from his briefcase and handed it to me – it was a petition for divorce.

It appeared that Ruth was so fed up with all the threats and bribery towards me and herself that she had reached breaking point and wanted to end the marriage.

The divorce proceedings were very unpleasant and demeaning to all the parties involved.

A decree absolute was granted, giving Ruth custody of the children with maintenance payments until their sixteenth birthdays. I was given open-ended access.

It seemed to me that my whole world had fallen in on me. There was nothing left of a twenty-five-year marriage, all because of the petty, vindictive behaviour of my fellow council members. For the next ten years I threw myself into my work.

Ruth and I were childhood sweethearts, so madly in love with each other, so the next few years were very traumatic.

It appears the enemy within were still doing their dirty work.

Relationships

THROUGH MY work, I met many people from all walks of life. Some were only interested in me for what I could do for them professionally or politically.

It was through my work that I met a young lady in the nursing profession. A relationship of some two years came to an end when I was invited for Sunday lunch to meet her family.

It was a lovely lunch and everyone enjoyed themselves. Then the bomb-shell was dropped. The young lady in question announced that she and I would be getting married in the very near future. What a shock! Marriage had never been on the agenda; I was seeking friendship, but obviously she had other ideas.

I thought I had had a lucky escape

and threw myself into even more work and meetings.

I soon got over the separation, and later became involved with a senior nurse at the local hospital. She was the same age as me and we shared, more or less, the same ideas about life. This relationship lasted some five years until one day, sitting in the office at the local ambulance station, the young lady in question burst into the office ranting and raving.

'You and I have got to get married!' she screamed. I thought to myself, Here we go again: wedding bells ringing; bottom drawer being planned.

So, that evening, she and I met to discuss the question of marriage. I had never raised the topic; obviously she was seeking a permanent and lasting relationship, and she never gave up. Every day she would bring up the subject and ask why marriage was not an option.

Eventually, she got the message and

the relationship came to an end. There were many more relationships with, just to mention a few, a matron, doctor, solicitor; all seeking my hand in marriage. I always maintained that you only love once, and my true love was Ruth.

End of Life

I NEVER GOT OVER my love for Ruth, my former wife. She was rehoused by the local council just a few hundred yards from the former matrimonial home and we often bumped into each other in town whilst shopping.

One day, whilst I was on duty at the local ambulance station, a 999 call was received: a female had collapsed in the street. On arrival, the paramedics found that the lady had suffered a massive heart attack and she was pronounced dead. Along with my children, I was informed of the sad news and was told that the deceased was none other than my ex-wife, Ruth. Everyone was devastated by the sad loss.

Life went on much the same, with me pursuing my mission in life for the poor and needy until one evening, sitting alone in the council chamber, I decided I had lost everything in life that was precious to me. I thought to myself, Now is the time for retirement from it all.

I resigned at the next elections for local government and informed the union of my intentions too. In the weeks that followed, I was still haunted by the enemy within. They were still up to their old tricks, making every effort to get me dismissed from the ambulance service.

In the end, during a reorganisation of the health service, I was selected for redundancy. This I accepted with some sadness, as I had devoted all of my working life to helping people and the ambulance service had given me the opportunity to fulfil some of my dreams and aspirations. I eventually took over the family undertaking business. I still work there to this day.

I maintain that you only love once.

This is very true as far as I am concerned. 'It is better to have loved and lost than never to have loved at all.' I have resigned myself to the fact that I will never marry again and have accepted that I will die a very lonely old man. I maintain that one can live with one's memories, and there are many in my life.

To conclude, it appears that the enemy within has won after all.

www.ingramcontent.com/pod-product-compliance
Lightning Source LLC
Chambersburg PA
CBHW051414250726

48655CB00003B/1041